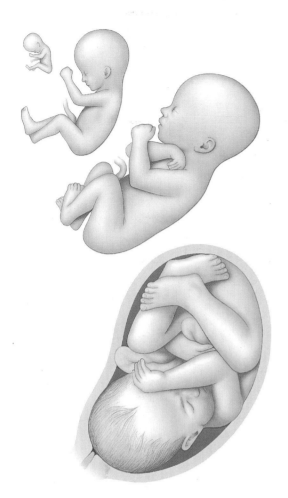

The Reproductive System

Steve Parker

RSVP®

RAINTREE STECK-VAUGHN
P U B L I S H E R S

The Steck-Vaughn Company

Austin, Texas

TITLES IN THE SERIES

**The Heart and Circulatory System
The Stomach and Digestive System
The Brain and Nervous System
The Lungs and Respiratory System
The Skeleton and Muscular System
The Reproductive System**

© Copyright 1998, text, Steck-Vaughn Company

HB 9/19/00 17.98L

Published by Raintree Steck-Vaughn Publishers,
an imprint of Steck-Vaughn Company

Library of Congress Cataloging-in-Publication Data
Parker, Steve.
The reproductive system / Steve Parker.
p.   cm.—(The human body)
Includes bibliographical references and index.
Summary: Explains the different parts of the reproductive system
and their functions and provides an overview of human development
from birth through adolescence
ISBN 0-8172-4806-4
1. Human reproduction system—Juvenile literature.
2. Generative organs—Juvenile literature.
[1. Reproduction. 2. Growth.]
I. Title. II. Series: Human body (Austin, Tex.)
QP251.5.P37   1997
612.6—dc21   96-29685

Printed in Italy. Bound in the United States.
1 2 3 4 5 6 7 8 9 0 02 01 00 99 98

Consultant: Dr. Tony Smith, Associate Editor of the British Medical Journal

Picture Acknowledgments
The publishers would like to thank the following for use of their photographs:
Sally & Richard Greenhill 8, 20; Lupe Cunha 11, 28, 38; National Medical Slide Bank 22;
Reflections 26, 27, 30; Science Photo Library 25, 35, 37, 40; Jennie Woodcock 33.
The remaining pictures are from the Wayland Picture Library.

CONTENTS

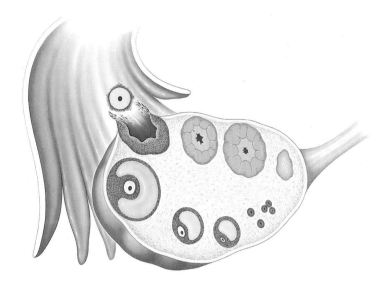

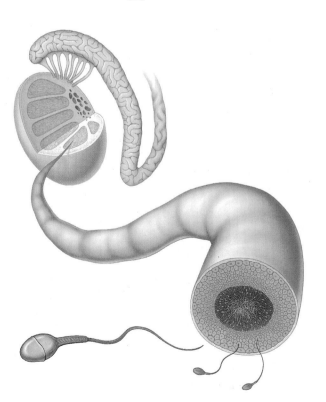

Introduction

The main feature of all living things is that they reproduce. That means they produce offspring, which are more living things very like themselves, and which continue their kind. Biologists include humans in the group of animals called mammals, because of our shared bodily features. These include warm blood, fur or hair on the skin, and the fact that, as part of reproduction, the mother usually feeds her new offspring on milk.

Humans have the same reproductive parts as other mammals. There are two sexes, female and male, or woman and man. They mate, or have sex. As a result, a tiny egg cell in the female may be joined, or fertilized, by a microscopic sperm cell from the male.

The fertilized egg grows and develops, in the mother's body, into a baby. This time of development is called pregnancy and lasts for nine months. The baby emerges into the world at birth and is fed on milk. The baby grows into an adult who can also reproduce, and so the cycle of life continues, generation after generation.

Added to this basic biology are our human features of intelligence, powers of thought, and very complex behavior. Attitudes about reproduction have varied enormously through time, and they vary enormously today, around the world. Societies and cultures have different attitudes, customs, and traditions. These involve various laws and regulations, religions, morals, types of partnerships, and basic human emotions and feelings. In different cultures, the facts of reproduction may also arouse embarrassment, discomfort, prejudice, and other strong views.

This book is less concerned with these views and feelings. It aims to describe and explain the biology of human reproduction, along with the main health care and medical topics linked to this most fundamental of life processes.

NOTE
The words and terms in this book follow standard scientific usage.

Family makeup varies with place, time, and individual circumstances. There may be one father, one mother, and several children. Or the mother may bring up a child on her own or a man may father children with several women. ▶

Female Reproductive System

The parts of the body concerned with reproduction are called the reproductive system. In a woman, they work together to produce pinhead-sized ripe eggs and to help a microscopic sperm cell from the man join with, or fertilize, one or more of these eggs. The reproductive system nourishes the fertilized egg as it develops into a baby, and when the baby is born provides milk for feeding.

The main parts or organs of the female reproductive system are in the woman's lower body, or **abdomen**. They include the ovaries, oviducts (also called uterine tubes or fallopian tubes), **uterus (womb)**, vagina (birth canal), vulva (external genitals), and the breasts on the upper body or chest.

The two ovaries are "egg-glands." They make and store the tiny eggs, or ova. Each of these, if fertilized by a sperm, develops into a baby. The ovaries also produce natural body chemicals called **hormones**, which control processes elsewhere in the body mainly concerning the female reproductive cycle (see page 8).

The two oviducts are thin tubes, one linking each **ovary** with the uterus. They carry the ripe eggs from the ovary to the uterus. When an egg is fertilized by a sperm, it usually happens in the oviduct.

The uterus is the place where the fertilized egg (sometimes more than one) grows and develops into a baby, ready to be born. The thick, muscular walls of the uterus can expand and stretch as the baby grows inside. When the female is not pregnant, the uterus is about the size of an elongated tennis ball. When she is pregnant with a fully grown baby, it is almost the size of a basketball. At birth, the baby leaves the uterus through its main opening, the neck (or cervix) and passes along the vagina (or birth canal) to the outside world.

The vagina, the uterus, and the passages inside the oviducts are all linked together and are known as the female reproductive tract. They are the pathway for eggs from the ovary to the uterus and for sperm coming in to fertilize an egg.

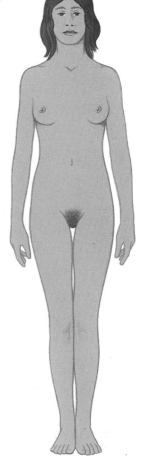

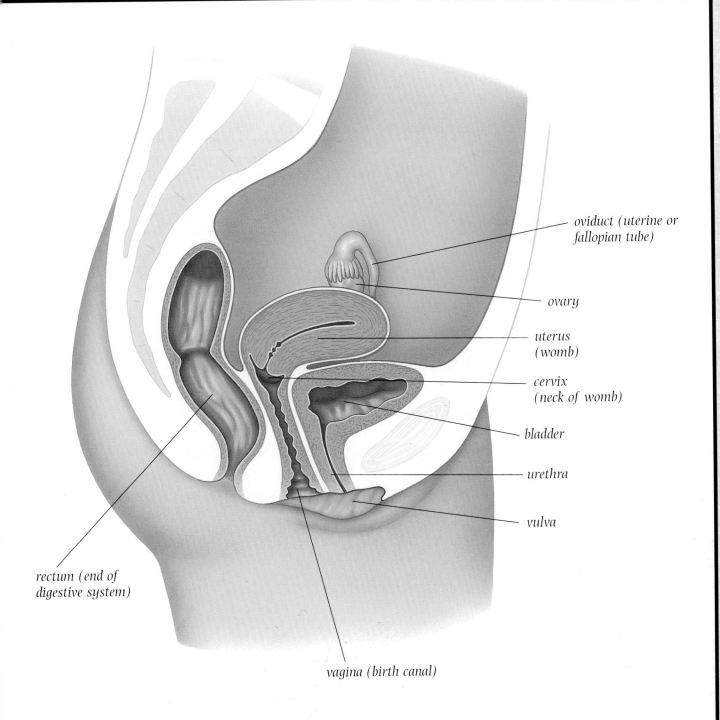

oviduct (uterine or
fallopian tube)

ovary

uterus
(womb)

cervix
(neck of womb)

bladder

urethra

vulva

rectum (end of
digestive system)

vagina (birth canal)

◄ Despite variations in dress and clothing, which change outer appearance, there are basic differences between the bodies of a woman and a man. Compared with a man (see page 12), a woman has a more rounded body shape, with narrower shoulders, wider hips, breasts on the chest, and little facial hair. These features are called secondary sexual characteristics.

▲ The female reproductive organs are sometimes called the genital organs. They have close links with the body's excretory or urinary system. For example, the opening of the vagina is just behind the opening of the urethra, the tube that conveys urine from the bladder to the outside. The two systems are described together as the urogenital or genitourinary system.

The Female Cycle

Awoman can become pregnant only at a certain time of the month. She can become pregnant only when she releases a fertile egg. The female reproductive system has a series of regular changes, the menstrual or reproductive cycle. The average cycle is 28 days. One egg from one ovary becomes ripe; then it is released from the ovary, ready to be fertilized by a sperm from the male. The uterus prepares to protect and nourish this fertilized egg as it grows into a baby. If **fertilization** happens, pregnancy begins, and the menstrual cycle ceases for several months. If fertilization does not happen, the egg is expelled, and the cycle begins again.

The menstrual cycle is controlled by hormones that are made by endocrine or hormonal **glands**. The glands release their hormones into

the blood, to circulate around the body. But each hormone affects only certain parts, called its target organs. The hormone controls the activity of its target organ by making it work faster or slower. The menstrual cycle involves four main hormones:

1. Follicle-stimulating hormone (FSH) is made in the pituitary gland, the pea-sized "master hormone gland" just under the brain. It stimulates an egg in the ovary to become ripe. It also encourages the egg's "container," or follicle, to make the hormone estrogen.

2. Luteinizing hormone (LH) also comes from the pituitary gland and encourages the egg follicle to make the hormone estrogen. LH then stimulates the egg to ripen fully and be ovulated, or released from the follicle, into the

◀ **The length of the menstrual cycle varies in different women, and in the same woman at different times. It can take 21 days or less, or 35 days or more. The cycle can be affected by general health, illness, lack of food, diet, stress, and depression. Menstrual cycles may be irregular, when they begin—between about 11 and 13—and when they stop, usually between 45 and 55.**

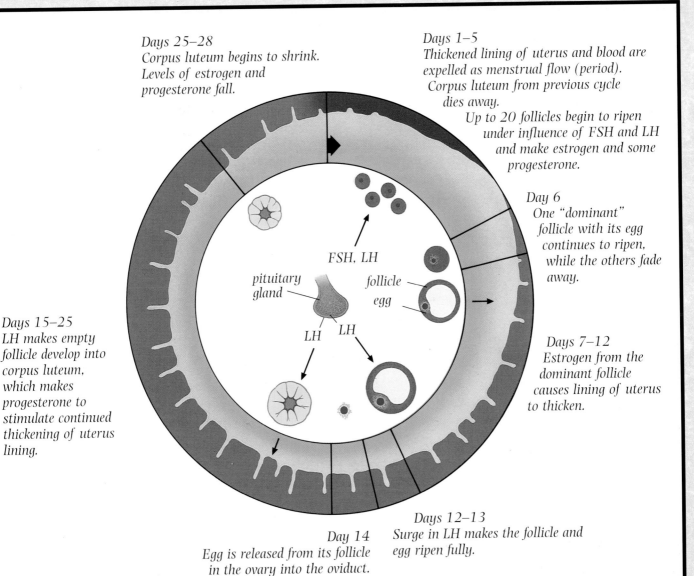

Days 25–28
Corpus luteum begins to shrink.
Levels of estrogen and
progesterone fall.

Days 1–5
Thickened lining of uterus and blood are
expelled as menstrual flow (period).
Corpus luteum from previous cycle
dies away.
Up to 20 follicles begin to ripen
under influence of FSH and LH
and make estrogen and some
progesterone.

Day 6
One "dominant"
follicle with its egg
continues to ripen,
while the others fade
away.

FSH, LH

pituitary
gland

follicle

egg

LH   LH

Days 15–25
LH makes empty
follicle develop into
corpus luteum,
which makes
progesterone to
stimulate continued
thickening of uterus
lining.

Days 7–12
Estrogen from the
dominant follicle
causes lining of uterus
to thicken.

Days 12–13
Surge in LH makes the follicle and
egg ripen fully.

Day 14
Egg is released from its follicle
in the ovary into the oviduct.

▲ If the egg is not fertilized, the thick,
nourishing lining of the uterus is not needed.
It breaks down and is expelled as a mixture of
blood and tissues from the vagina. This is the
menstrual flow (menses or period), and it
usually lasts from three to five days. Then the
cycle begins again.

oviduct. It stimulates the empty follicle to
become a small yellowish body, the corpus
luteum.

3. Estrogen is the main female hormone. It is
made in the ripening egg follicle and also in the
corpus luteum when the egg has been released.
Estrogen stimulates the egg to ripen further,
and it makes the lining of the uterus thick and
rich with blood, ready to nourish the egg if it is
fertilized. This hormone also causes the general
female features of the whole body.

4. Progesterone is the second major female
hormone. It is made in the ripening follicles
and the corpus luteum. It stimulates the uterus
lining to become even thicker and ready to
nourish the egg if it is fertilized.

Making Eggs

Human life begins with two microscopic **cells**, the egg or **ovum** of the mother, and the sperm or **spermatozoon** of the father. Each of these contains a half-set of the DNA-based genes, the chemical codes for building a new human body (see page 26). When an egg and sperm join at fertilization, they form a complete set of genes, and the baby begins its development from this fertilized egg.

The ovary contains many thousands of unripe or immature eggs, known as primary oocytes. Each one is inside a group of other cells called the primordial **follicle**. The follicle cells support and nourish the egg cell, and they also make the female hormone estrogen. These unripe or primordial follicles are microscopic.

Usually, one egg and its follicle develop and ripen during each menstrual cycle. This may be one egg from alternate ovaries each time, but not always. An immature egg cell is about 30 micrometers (0.03 millimeters) across, which is almost invisible to the unaided eye, but relatively large for a body cell. When it has fully ripened into a secondary oocyte and is

▼ **These pictures show the development and ripening of an egg cell (oocyte) in its blisterlike container, the follicle. The process takes about 12–14 days, which is the first half of the menstrual cycle. The empty follicle becomes a corpus luteum during the third phase of the cycle, and then fades away if there is no pregnancy.**

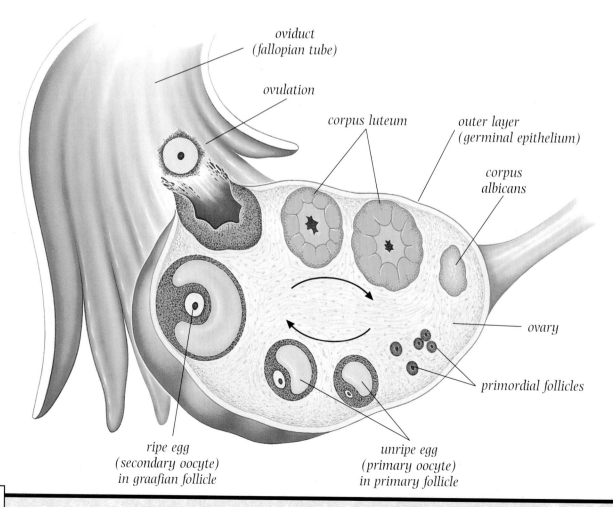

oviduct
(fallopian tube)

ovulation

corpus luteum

outer layer
(germinal epithelium)

corpus
albicans

ovary

primordial follicles

ripe egg
(secondary oocyte)
in graafian follicle

unripe egg
(primary oocyte)
in primary follicle

ready to be released, it is ten times as big as the primary egg cell. The follicle around it has developed to about two millimeters across, much of this being fluid. It is known as a graafian follicle, and it looks like a small blister on the surface of the ovary.

These changes take place under the control of various hormones, as described on the previous pages. At **ovulation**, the follicle "pops" and releases its fluid and ripe egg. The egg floats into the wide, trumpet-shaped end of the oviduct and begins its journey along this tube.

The empty follicle shrinks slightly, and the cells in its lining multiply to form a corpus luteum. This is, in effect, a tiny and temporary hormone gland, as small as a rice grain.

▲ **Sometimes an ovary releases more than one egg, or both ovaries release an egg at the same time. If these eggs are fertilized, this can lead to a multiple birth—such as twins, triplets, and so on. Since more than one egg is involved, they will not be identical.**

FACT BOX

• The egg cells multiply in numbers very early in life. Before a baby girl is even born, she has about one million egg cells in each ovary.

• By about ten years of age, most of these have died, leaving around 50,000 to 100,000 in each ovary.

• About 20 eggs in their follicles begin to ripen at the start of each menstrual period. But usually only one becomes dominant and continues. The rest die.

• Through the average woman's reproductive time, about 400–500 egg cells become ripe and are ovulated.

The corpus luteum makes mainly progesterone, the hormone that stimulates the uterus lining to become thick and well supplied with blood. Progesterone also prepares the milk or mammary glands in the breasts to make milk for the possible pregnancy. If the egg is not fertilized, the corpus luteum shrinks and fades away into a very tiny knot of pale scar tissue, the corpus albicans (white body). As a woman gets older, these accumulate around the outside of the ovary, one for each ovulation.

Male Reproductive System

The parts of the male reproductive system work together to produce microscopic tadpole-shaped sperm and to release these sperm into the reproductive system of the female during sexual intercourse.

The main parts or **organs** of the system are in or just below the lower body, or abdomen. They include the **testes** (testicles) and the coiled tubes of the epididymides, hanging in a skin bag, the scrotum. Other parts are the sperm ducts (also called the ductus deferens or vas deferens), prostate gland and other glands, and the penis containing a tube, the urethra.

The testes are "sperm-glands." They are the equivalent of the ovaries in the female. (Both ovaries and testes are also known as the main reproductive organs, or gonads.) The testes make and store the tiny sperm cells, spermatozoa. They also produce hormones, especially the chief male hormone, testosterone. This stimulates the production of sperm cells and also causes the general male features of the body.

Each epididymis is a set of tightly coiled tubes lying alongside the testis. It helps sperm to become mature and stores them. The sperm ducts are thin tubes that carry the ripe sperm away from the testes and epididymides, toward the outside. The sperm ducts join together and also join another tube called the urethra, inside a small gland, the prostate. The urethra carries the sperm through the penis, to the outside.

The fluid-filled passageways inside the testes, epididymides, sperm ducts, and urethra are all linked together. They are the pathway for sperm on their way to the outside. They are known as the male reproductive tract.

Compared with an average woman (see ▲ page 6), an average man has a more angular body shape, with more pronounced muscles, broader shoulders, narrower hips, hairy chest, and facial hair. These features are called secondary sexual characteristics. As with the female characteristics, these features vary from one person to another.

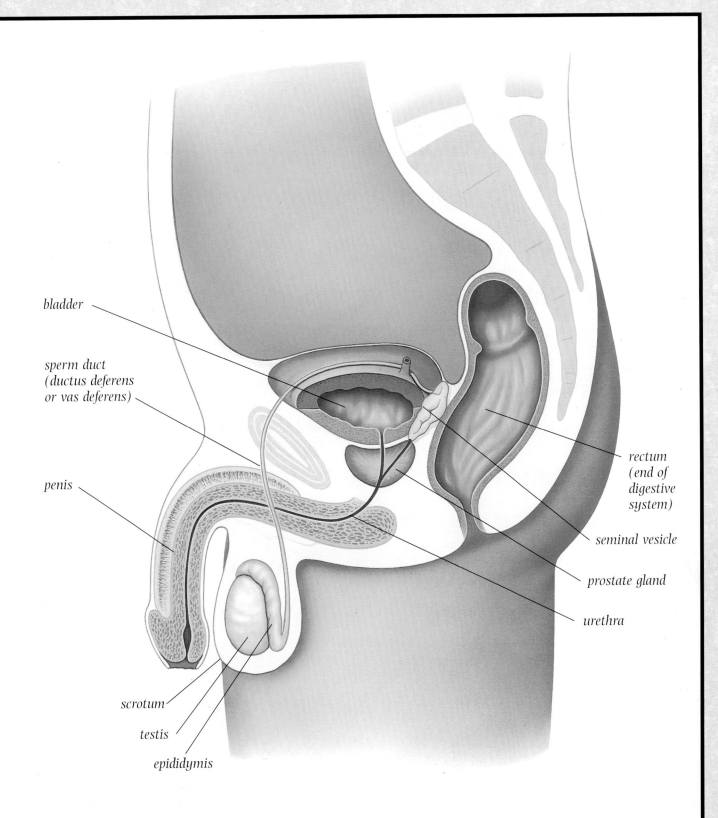

bladder

sperm duct
(ductus deferens
or vas deferens)

penis

scrotum

testis

epididymis

rectum
(end of
digestive
system)

seminal vesicle

prostate gland

urethra

▲ **The male reproductive organs are sometimes called the genital organs. Like the female reproductive organs, they have close links with the excretory or urinary system. For example, the tube that carries sperm along the penis to the outside, the urethra, also conveys urine from the bladder. The two systems are sometimes described together as the urogenital or genitourinary system.**

Making Sperm

The female sex cells are eggs, and each month an egg ripens. In a man, the process is very different. The sex cells are the sperm, and millions of them are formed every day, in a continuous production line inside the testes.

The testes hang between the legs inside a skin bag, the scrotum. Each testis is a coiled bundle of some 900 tiny tubes called seminiferous tubules. If they were all joined together, they would be more than 650 ft. (200 m) long. Inside each seminiferous tubule is a lining of cells called spermatogonia. These are multiplying every minute, producing slightly smaller cells known as spermatocytes, which collect on the inner sides of the spermatogonia.

Over several days, each spermatocyte gradually changes shape. It shrinks and grows a short tail, making it look like a dumpy tadpole.

Gradually the tail lengthens and the head becomes even smaller. The spermatocyte becomes a spermatid, which is an almost fully mature sperm. By now, the spermatid has moved near the middle of the seminiferous tubule, as more spermatocytes are formed.

Finally, the spermatids loosen and move into the fluid in the middle of the tubule. Then they move along the tubule to its end. Millions of them from hundreds of tubules finally pass into another set of coiled tubes lying next to the testis. This is the epididymis; straightened out it would measure about 20 ft. (6 m). The sperm are stored in the epididymis and become fully mature spermatozoa.

In the male reproductive system, several glands make fluids that are added to the sperm when they are released. They include the prostate gland and the two seminal vesicles. The fluids are called semen. They contain sugars and other energy-rich chemicals to nourish the sperm, and various substances to stimulate the sperm and make them swim.

FACT BOX

• A sperm takes about four weeks to grow and mature.

• The whole sperm, including the tail, is only 50 micrometers (0.05 millimeters) long, and its head is just 2.5 micrometers (0.0025 millimeters) wide. In fact, sperm are among the smallest cells in the body.

• About 300 million sperm cells become mature each day.

• If sperm are not released, they live for about one month. Then they die and their parts are absorbed back into the body for recycling.

The continuous production line inside ▶
the seminiferous tubule begins with
spermatogonia. These divide to make
spermatocytes, which develop into spermatids
and finally into mature sperm (spermatozoa).
Sperm pass from the mass of coiled
seminiferous tubules into the epididymis for
final maturation and storage.

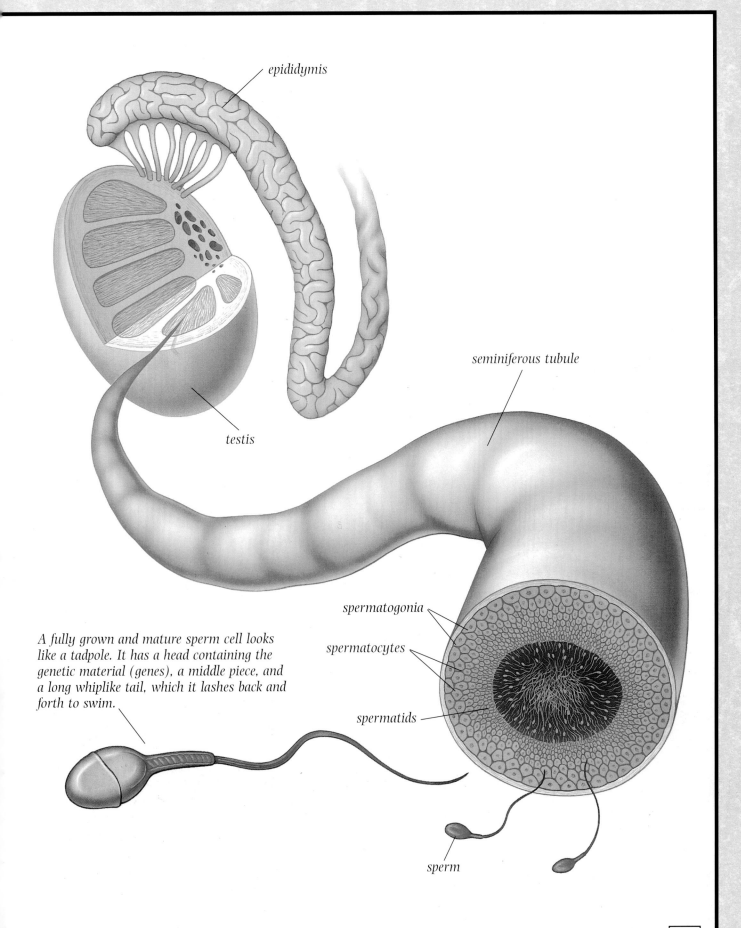

epididymis

seminiferous tubule

testis

spermatogonia

spermatocytes

spermatids

A fully grown and mature sperm cell looks like a tadpole. It has a head containing the genetic material (genes), a middle piece, and a long whiplike tail, which it lashes back and forth to swim.

sperm

Egg Meets Sperm

The key event in reproduction is fertilization, the coming together of an egg from a woman and a sperm from a man. The two cells join to form one cell, the fertilized egg. This brings together the two half-sets of genetic material carried by the egg and sperm, to form a complete set of genes (see page 36). The process of fertilization and the settling of the fertilized egg into the uterus are called conception, or conceiving a baby.

▼ Tiny sperm cells swarm around the egg cell, dwarfed by its huge size. At fertilization, one sperm pushes its head onto the surface of the egg. The casing of the sperm head and the membrane around the egg join. This allows the genetic material inside the sperm's head to pass into the egg cell, where it can link up with the egg's genetic material. Then a thick barrier, the zona pellucida, forms around the fertilized egg, to keep out other sperm.

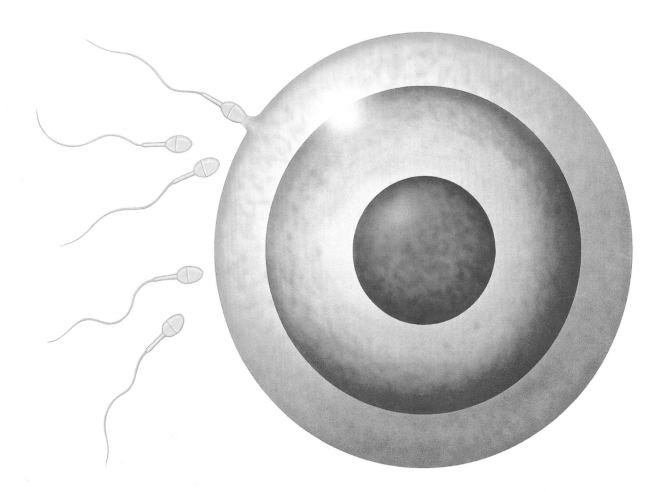

Feelings and emotions such as love, attraction, and sexual desire can happen at almost any time. But the biological side of sex—conceiving a baby—is more limited. Fertilization can happen only if the egg is recently released from the ovary (ovulated) and if the sperm have recently arrived in the female reproductive tract, since they live for only a few days there. This means a woman can conceive a baby during part of her reproductive cycle, during the "fertile period," which is usually within a few days of ovulation.

For fertilization to occur, the sperm must be able to reach the egg, which is usually in the oviduct. The sperm get from the male reproductive tract to the female reproductive tract by the process of sexual intercourse, or sex. The man and the woman become sexually aroused and the man's penis becomes pumped up by blood and is longer, larger, and stiffer; this is an erection. The lining of the woman's vagina makes fluid so it is slippery; this is lubrication. The man pushes his erect penis into the vagina of the woman; this is penetration. The penis moves back and forth in the vagina, and the man releases his sperm; this is ejaculation. Ejaculation happens when muscular contractions in his reproductive tract pump the sperm from the epididymides and

sperm ducts into the urethra, where they are joined by seminal fluids from the prostate and other glands. Some 300–500 million sperm, in about 3–5 milliliters of fluid, pass along the urethra, out of the end of the penis, and into the vagina.

The sperm must swim about 8 in. (20 cm) from the vagina, into the cervix or neck of the uterus, and through the hollow uterus, into the oviducts. Millions perish on the way or take a wrong turn and go into the oviduct, where there is no egg. Perhaps a few tens of thousands reach the ripe egg in the other oviduct, but it takes only one of these sperm to join with or fertilize the egg.

The Fertilized Egg

The fertilized egg drifts slowly through the fluid in the oviduct, toward the uterus. The journey takes about four or five days. During this time, the egg is already beginning its development. About 36 hours after fertilization, the egg splits down the middle, by the process of cell division, to produce two cells. Some 12 hours later, each of these cells divides again, making four cells. These cells then divide again and again about every 12 hours.

This early stage of development is called **cleavage**. It does not involve growth. The original egg was a relatively huge cell, more than 100 micrometers (0.1 millimeters) across. It contained stored nutrients to survive during cleavage, since it gets no nourishment from other sources. As the cells split in half, in half again, and so on, they become smaller, until they are once again about the same size as ordinary body cells.

By the third or fourth set of cell divisions, the splitting process gets random and disordered. Some four days after fertilization, the result is a tiny blackberry-like ball of around 50 to 80 cells, called the morula. It finishes its journey along the oviduct and enters the hollow chamber inside the uterus (womb).

The cells of the morula continue to divide, forming a hollow ball with fluid inside, called the blastocyst. By now, the nutrients in the original egg cell are running low. About one week after fertilization, the blastocyst burrows itself into the lining of the uterus, called the endometrium. This is thickened and rich with blood, as part of the menstrual cycle. The blastocyst actually "eats" its way into the lining and begins to absorb nutrients from it, for further growth. This burrowing is known as implantation.

During the menstrual cycle, the thickened lining of the uterus begins to break down about two weeks after ovulation. But if an egg is fertilized and develops into a blastocyst, the outer cells of the blastocyst produce a hormone called hCG (human chorionic gonadotrophin). This hormone keeps the corpus luteum, back in the ovary, producing the hormones estrogen and progesterone. In turn, these hormones keep the lining of the uterus thickened and rich with nourishing blood, so the blastocyst can implant into the uterus. The regular menstrual cycle is altered, and there is no menstrual flow. This missed period is an early sign of pregnancy.

The fertilized egg is a giant cell. As it ▶ divides into two cells, then four, and so on, the sizes of the resulting cells get smaller, until they are back to normal body cell size. About a week after egg and sperm join, they become a blastocyst and tunnel into the uterus lining for protection and nourishment.

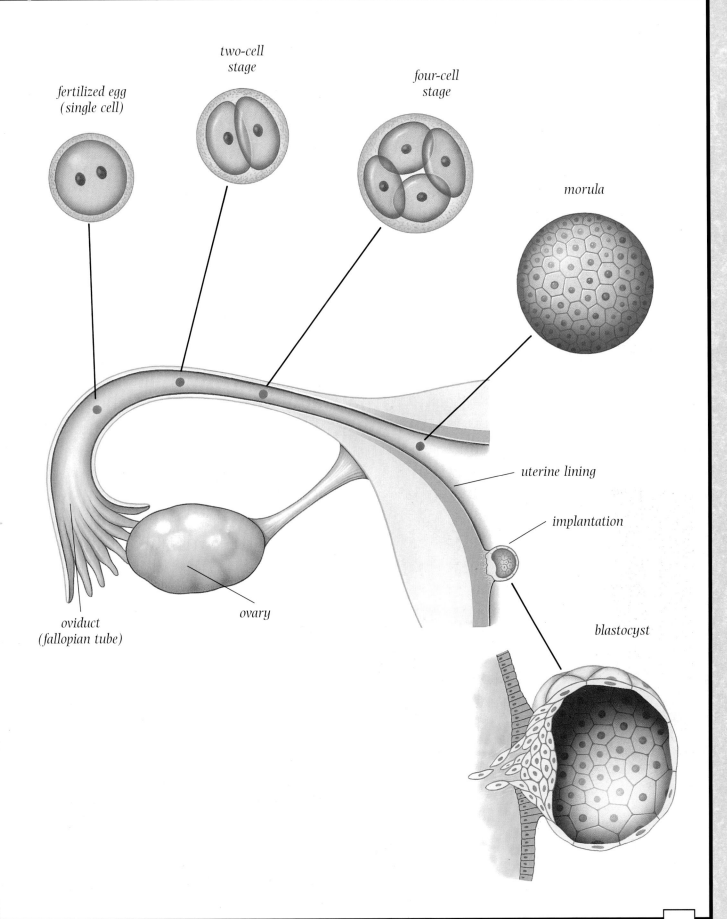

fertilized egg
(single cell)

two-cell
stage

four-cell
stage

morula

uterine lining

implantation

oviduct
(fallopian tube)

ovary

blastocyst

The Developing Embryo

As the pinhead-sized blastocyst settles into the lining of the uterus, its cells take in nourishment. They continue to multiply, move around, and differentiate, or become slightly different from each other. This is the embryonic stage of development and lasts for eight weeks following fertilization.

The inner cells form a flattened circular shape, the embryonic disk, which will develop into the baby. The outer cells organize themselves into thin ball-like layers. These will become the thin membranes, including the amnion, around the baby. The outer cells also form a small, yellowish yolk sac. This contains nutrients for the second and third weeks after fertilization. Having provided nourishment for a short period, the yolk sac then shrinks away. The yolk sac is much bigger in birds and reptiles than in humans.

The cells of the embryonic disk multiply thousands of times. They also move to new positions and places and change into more specialized cells. Gradually the **embryo** takes shape. Its cells form the main body systems, such as the brain and nerves, heart and blood, stomach and intestines, muscles and skin. Eight weeks after fertilization, the embryo is still only about the size of an adult human's thumb. Yet all of its main parts and organs have formed, and its heart is beating.

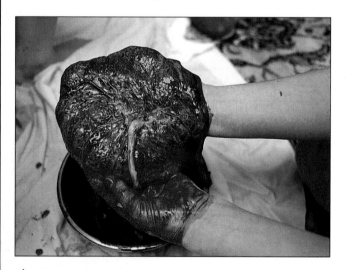

▲ Some of the cells around the embryonic disk multiply and form tiny fingerlike shapes in the uterus lining, surrounded by pools of the mother's blood. This will become the placenta. Its job is to pass nutrients from the mother's blood to the baby's blood. The baby's blood flows back and forth between its body and the placenta along the umbilical cord. The placenta also makes hormones, including hCG, which continues to prevent the menstrual cycle so that pregnancy can continue.

The change from a blackberry-like ball of ▶ cells into a tiny human body depends on three processes. These processes are cell multiplication, differentiation, and migration. It takes only about six weeks, and never again will the body grow so fast.

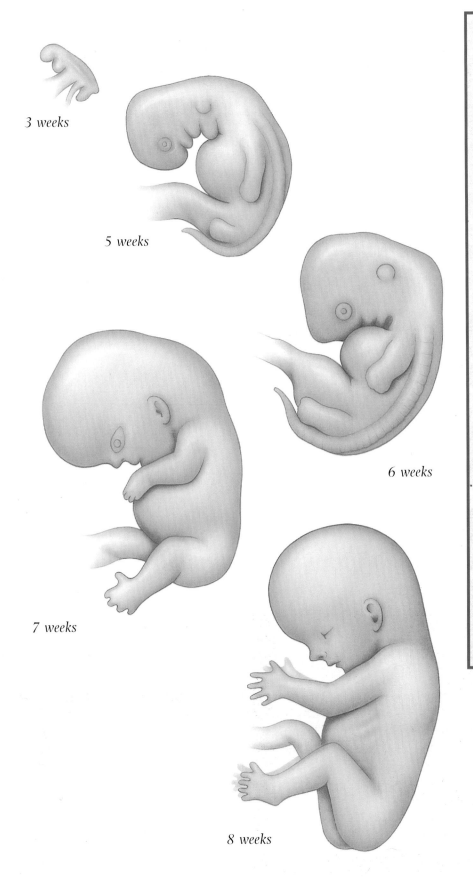

3 weeks

5 weeks

6 weeks

7 weeks

8 weeks

THE CHANGING EMBRYO

- *Third week after fertilization*
  Head of the embryo can be identified from the body
  Heart begins to pulsate
- *Fourth week after fertilization*
  Tiny limbs begin to grow out as bulges or buds
  Stomach and guts form as a simple tube
- *Fifth week after fertilization*
  Brain grows rapidly
  Nose starts to form
  Early muscles form in the head, body, and limbs
- *Sixth week after fertilization*
  Ears and eyes are more obvious
  Body becomes straighter
- *Seventh week after fertilization*
  Face and neck take shape
  Fingers and toes form
  Tail begins to shrink
- *Eighth week after fertilization*
  All main body parts formed
  Details such as eyelids being added
  Embryo looks recognizably human

The Growing Fetus

After the embryonic phase of development, the baby progresses to the next stage. This is the fetal phase, which lasts from nine weeks after fertilization through to birth. The baby is no longer called an embryo. It is called a **fetus**.

The main changes during this time are growth in overall body size and addition of the "finishing touches," such as fingernails and toenails to the body. These changes take place in the same way as the earlier embryonic development, as cells multiply, move, and differentiate.

The fetus floats in a pool of amniotic fluid inside the uterus. It is surrounded by the amniotic **membrane**. The fluid and membrane cushion the fetus from bumps, jolts, and loud noises as the mother moves about. The fetus cannot breathe by itself to obtain oxygen or eat any food. All its oxygen and nourishment come from the mother's blood, via the placenta. The baby's blood continues to flow back and forth from its body to the placenta along the umbilical cord.

A woman can tell if she is pregnant in various ways. The missed menstrual period is an early clue, though a period can be delayed or missed for other reasons. Sometimes she "just knows." A chemical pregnancy test detects the hormone hCG, which is first made by the outer cells of the blastocyst and then by the placenta in much larger quantities. hCG gets into the mother's urine and blood and can be picked up in a pregnancy test. A mother-to-be also may have various pregnancy checkups, carried out by doctors and health workers. The ultrasound scan "sees" into the uterus by using high-pitched sound waves. It is usually carried out around the 16th to 18th week of pregnancy, to check that the fetus is healthy and is developing normally. It also provides an accurate measure of the baby's age, so the day of birth can be calculated.

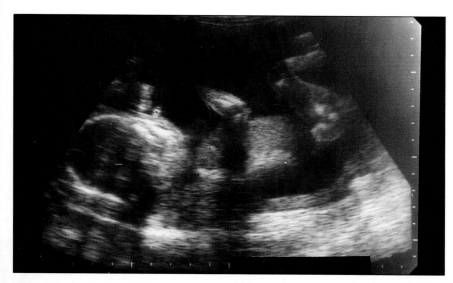

◀ This ultrasound scan shows a baby about 16 weeks old lying on its back in the womb. The head is on the left, one arm sticks upward, and the leg is raised on the right.

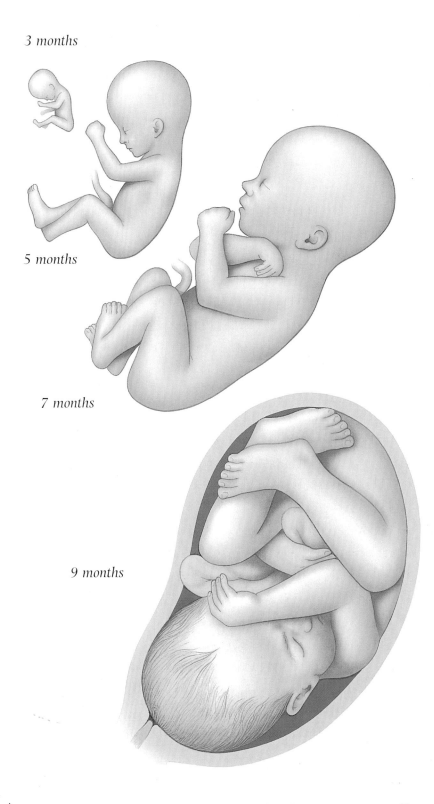

3 months

5 months

7 months

9 months

▲ **In the middle phase of pregnancy, the fetus grows rapidly. The muscular wall of the uterus gradually stretches to accommodate it.**

THE GROWING FETUS

- *Third month*
Bones begin to form
Intestines loop around into coil
Kidneys start to work
- *Fourth month*
Cheeks, nose, lips, and facial
  features are more shaped
Sex organs show if baby will be
  boy or girl
Mother can feel her uterus
  becoming bigger
- *Fifth month*
Hair grows on the head
Most bones have taken shape
Fetus can grip, kick, and hiccup
- *Sixth month*
The fetus loses its round shape
  and becomes leaner
Nostrils open
Fetus may suck its thumb
- *Seventh month*
Eyelids open
Eyes react to bright light filtering
  through into uterus
Fetus may attempt breathing and
  swallowing movements
- *Eighth month*
Fetus becomes rounder
Tongue can taste
Finger and toe nails almost
  grown
- *Ninth month*
Fine lanugo or "baby hair" falls
  out
Inside the uterus the fetus usually
  turns over, head-down, ready to
  be born

Birth

Birth is a momentous event for baby and mother. The first stage is called labor, and the following order of events varies from one mother to another.

The fully grown baby's head presses down on the cervix, the muscular neck of the uterus. This has been tightly closed during pregnancy, but it begins to relax and widen, ready to allow the baby through.

THE LENGTH OF PREGNANCY

• "Birthday" is sometimes thought of as the baby's first day of life. But the baby has already been growing and developing for months inside the mother's uterus.
• The average time for a human pregnancy is 266 days, from fertilization of the egg by the sperm to birth.
• However, the timing of pregnancy, and calculating the due date for the birth, is usually taken from the first day of the menstrual cycle before the pregnancy. (This is the day when the last period began.)
• An average cycle is 28 days, and ovulation and fertilization usually occur in the middle. This gives an extra 14 days.
• So there is a total of 280 days from the first day of the last menstrual cycle to the day of birth.

During pregnancy, the cervix has been sealed by a plug of sticky **mucus**. This loosens and comes out through the mother's birth canal, or vagina. It is called the "show." Also the amnion and other membranes around the baby split, releasing the amniotic fluid. When this happens we say "the waters broke."

The walls of the uterus are made of very strong muscles. These begin to shorten in rhythmic contractions, stimulated by the hormone oxytocin, made in the pituitary gland of the mother. The contractions put pressure on the baby and squeeze it through the widening cervix. The mother feels them as uncomfortable or painful spasms.

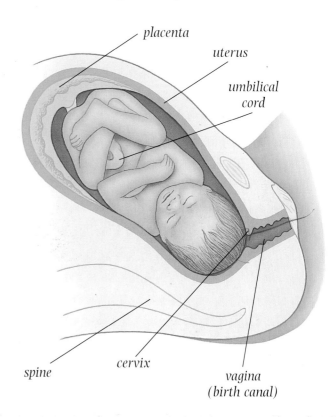

placenta

uterus

umbilical cord

spine

cervix

vagina (birth canal)

Usually, after several hours of uterine contractions, the cervix widens, or dilates, enough to allow the baby through. The second stage of birth, delivery, follows. The contractions gradually push the baby out of the uterus, through the cervix, and along the birth canal toward the outside world. The head is the widest part of the new baby, and most babies are born headfirst.

The third stage is delivery of the placenta, or afterbirth. The uterus continues its contractions and squeezes out the placenta, which has come away from its inner lining, along with the membranes and fluids. Meanwhile the newborn may cry loudly. This helps clear the baby's lungs of fluid and start its breathing. The infant may also take its first milk from the mother's breast. Birth is exhausting, and mother and baby settle down to rest.

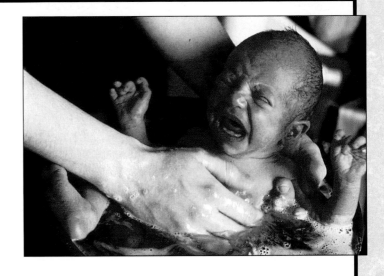

▲   Inside the uterus, the baby cannot breathe or eat. As it is born, the infant begins to breathe air and may cry loudly to expand the lungs and clear them of fluid. Blood flow to the placenta stops. The main blood flow to the lungs begins to collect oxygen. Blood flow to the baby's digestive system also increases, to collect nutrients from the first meal of milk.

▼   During the journey out of the uterus or womb, and along the birth canal, the baby's head generally turns sideways, allowing it to fit more easily through the oval hole in the mother's pelvis.

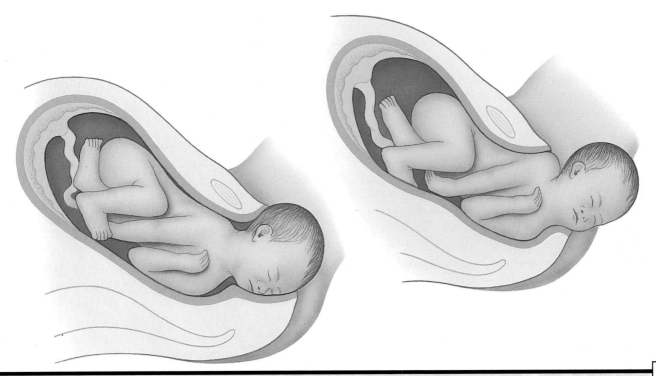

The Newborn

The first few hours and days after birth are extremely important for the baby and its mother, and usually the father too. Touching and cuddling are very natural actions that help them to get to know each other. This process is called bonding and happens especially when the mother nurses her baby.

Both baby and mother soon learn to recognize each other by their distinctive sights, sounds, and smells. Newborn babies cannot see distant objects clearly at first; they can only see details of objects up to about 16 in. (40 cm) away. So they are, in effect, "nearsighted."

Babies can hear fairly well. They are soothed by quiet, relaxed sounds and upset by loud, sharp noises. But they need time to learn about the details of sounds, the directions they come from, and how to turn the head to look for the source of the sound—which is something we do almost without thinking.

◀ **Mother and baby take a peaceful rest, relax, and get to know each other—even though they have been in extremely close contact for many months.**

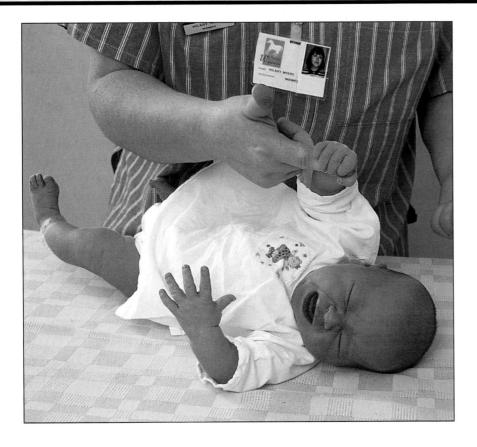

In most countries, a doctor or nurse examines a new baby and carries out health checks. They weigh and measure each baby, check the face, head, body, and limbs, listen to the heart and lungs, and test the reflexes or automatic reactions. Here the reflex test involves gripping. The nurse checks how tightly the baby can grip her thumb.

Smell is very important at this stage too, though mother and baby may not realize it at the time. Within hours, they both come to know each other's distinctive body smells. If a baby several days old is held by another new mother, not its own, it may become restless and start crying—partly because the smells are different.

A newborn is a "bundle of reflexes." A reflex is an automatic reaction of the body to a stimulus. For several stimuli, such as being too hot or cold, being very hungry or in pain, the baby has one main reaction: it cries.

In some cases, mother or baby have problems during birth. There are many causes, from some kind of medical illness, to a very large baby and a small mother, or just to sheer exhaustion. There are various ways to help. One is to deliver the baby with forceps. A forceps is an instrument that "grabs" the baby's head and helps ease it from the womb. Another way to get the baby out is a Cesarean section. A surgical cut is made through the mother's abdomen into the womb, and the baby emerges through this incision.

FACT BOX

• Around the world, about 170 babies are born every minute.

• The country with the most births each year—and the most people—is China. About 25 babies are born every minute.

• The birth rate compares births to population size. It is the number of babies born per 1,000 people in a country or region, per year. In the early 1990s the birth rate was highest in Malawi in Africa, at about 50 babies per 1,000 people per year. Lowest was San Marino, a tiny republic in Italy, at 9.5.

Infancy

A human body grows faster during the first nine months inside the womb, and then during its first year, than at any other time in its life. In countries such as Great Britain, the United States, and Australia, average weight at birth is between 6.5 and 8.8 lbs. (3 and 4 kg). By the end of the first year, a well-fed baby increases its body weight to between 17 and 24 lbs. (8 and 11 kg) —almost three times the birth weight.

A newborn baby's brain is about one-third of its eventual adult weight. By the age of one year, the brain has increased to two-thirds of its adult weight. Along with this amazing growth comes an incredible amount of learning and development. A baby learns to smile, lift its head from a lying position, roll over when lying, and sit up—all within about 6 to 7 months. These are easy tasks for grownups. But the baby needs great effort, coordination, and concentration to achieve them. By the end of the first year, most babies can say a few simple words and walk a few unsteady steps.

These various stages of development, such as sitting, crawling, walking, and talking, are sometimes called milestones. These milestones happen at different times in different babies, though they usually happen in the same order in most babies. If a baby seems slightly slow to

▶ **A young child learns by trial and error. He or she tries a movement or manipulation and watches to see the result. Gradually, physical skills are learned and improved.**

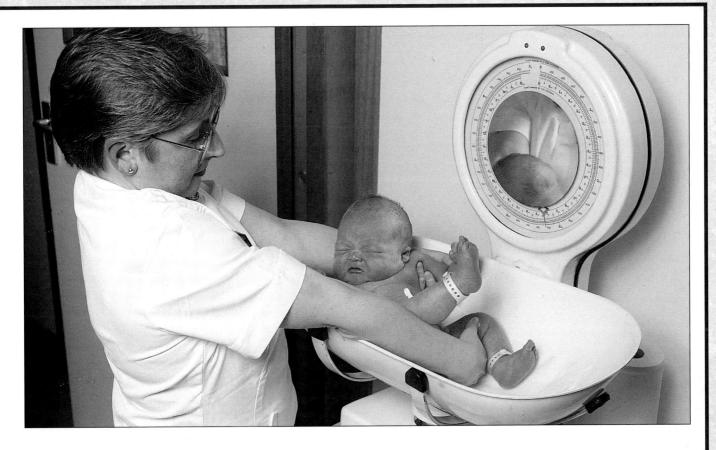

▲ **At a postnatal (after birth) checkup, a nurse makes sure all is well.**

develop or learn, it is usually no cause for concern. It does not necessarily mean that she or he will lag behind in the future. The baby will probably soon catch up.

However, in rare cases there may be problems. That is why babies and their parents are advised to have regular checkups. The doctor or nurse can examine and weigh the baby, carry out various tests on vision, hearing, and muscle coordination, and make sure that all is well.

The body protects itself against infectious diseases caused by germs, such as viruses and bacteria, in many ways. One way is by developing substances called antibodies, which circulate in the blood. When a certain type of germ gets into the body, the antibodies against that germ attach themselves to it and disable or kill it.

There are antibodies against some germs in the mother's breast milk. A breast-fed baby takes these in, to gain some protection in the early stages of life.

Many countries carry out immunizations, or vaccinations. This involves giving a baby or child a weakened version of the germ, as an injection or as a liquid or food. The germ cannot cause the disease, but it does cause the baby's body to produce antibodies against it. The baby is then protected against that disease for the future.

There are immunizations against diphtheria, tetanus, pertussis (whooping cough), polio, measles, mumps, rubella (German measles), tuberculosis, and other infections. However, the exact choice and timing of immunizations vary from place to place and according to each baby's health and medical condition.

Childhood

▲ **At playschool children play and have fun. At the same time they are learning basic physical and mental skills and also social skills and awareness of others.**

As a baby grows into a toddler, and then into a child, development and learning continue at a rapid rate. Some of the learning is obvious. It's done during regular lessons, starting at nursery schools and playgroups, and continues in school classrooms for ten years or more. Children learn many tasks, including counting, drawing, reading, and writing.

There are many other kinds of learning. Children learn how to walk, run, and jump with greater skill. They learn how to play organized games such as soccer, baseball, and tennis—not only the movements and actions, but also the rules and tactics. They may learn complicated physical skills such as playing a musical instrument, painting, or dancing.

There are even more kinds of learning. Some learning happens without actual lessons, even unconsciously. Children learn how to play, have fun, and enjoy themselves. They learn how to make friends—and perhaps enemies. Each child also develops her or his likes, dislikes, ideas, opinions, and personality.

Throughout childhood the body continues to grow. The muscles become more coordinated, and this allows more skilled actions such as threading a needle or drawing tiny details in a picture.

◀ One important area of learning involves keeping the body clean and healthy. Washing away dirt and sweat helps prevent skin spots, sores, and rashes. Cleaning teeth is another important hygiene skill, but it may be awkward to do at first.

Female Adolescence

During childhood, girls and boys grow in a similar way. On the average, they are about the same height and weight. With the same training and opportunities, their physical skills can also be similar.

From about the age of 10 to 12, girls and boys begin to grow differently. For most girls, this is the beginning of **puberty**, a time of rapid physical growth and bodily development, when the sexual organs start to mature and function. Before this age, the body's reproductive parts are present, but some of them are relatively small, and they do not work. At puberty a girl's body begins to change into the body of a woman.

In most girls puberty is complete by the age of about 15 to 17. But it is also part of a large-scale process called **adolescence**. For both girls and boys, this involves becoming physically and sexually mature. Adolescence can also include changes in moods, emotions, likes, dislikes, outlook, friendships, relationships, and many other aspects of behavior and personality.

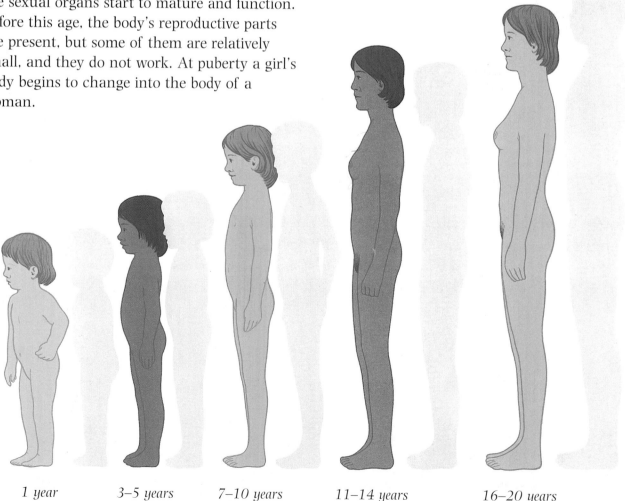

1 year   *3–5 years*   *7–10 years*   *11–14 years*   *16–20 years*

▲ **Young adolescent girls often group together and follow the same interests and fashions, such as clothes, foods, sports, and music. Boys do the same. The sexes tend to stay separate until boy-girl relationships develop during later adolescence.**

Adolescence is not only physical but also cultural. In some societies it is traditionally kept quiet, even ignored. In some regions, it is accepted in a matter-of-fact, everyday way, without worry or fanfare. In other places, it is a time of great celebration when a female can conceive her own babies. The passing of childhood and the arrival of adulthood is often marked with a celebration or special event.

◄ **This chart shows the average height with age for girls in developed countries such as Great Britain or the United States. Puberty involves a spurt in growth, when height increases rapidly for a few years.**

The main changes of puberty are under the control of hormones, especially estrogen and progesterone. They include
• rapid growth of the bones and the rest of the body, with a rapid increase in height.
• development of pads of fat and connective tissue, which produce the more rounded body shape of a woman, compared with the angular contours of a young girl.
• appearance of thicker, more conspicuous body hairs under the arms and pubic hair between the legs.
• development of the breasts and growth and maturing of the female sexual organs.
• the start of the menstrual cycle and the monthly period. The cycle is often irregular at the beginning. The first full cycle and period is called menarche. It usually happens when a girl reaches 100 to 105 lbs. (45–48 kg), rather than at a certain height or age, although for most, menarche occurs between 11 and 14 years.

Male Adolescence

Most boys begin the growth spurt and sexual development of puberty from the ages of 12 to 14. The genital organs become larger, the testes begin to make sperm, and the glands produce their various fluids.

For males, the time of puberty finishes around the ages of 17 to 18. By this stage, the typical male body is almost fully grown and sexually mature. The boy's body has changed into a man's, and he can have sexual intercourse and become a father.

At this stage the male body is also approaching its peak of basic physical fitness. However, many people involved in physical activities such as athletics and sports continue to improve. They practice, refine their muscle and coordination skills, work on their mental attitudes and approaches, and develop their tactical abilities. This often means their best performances are still to come.

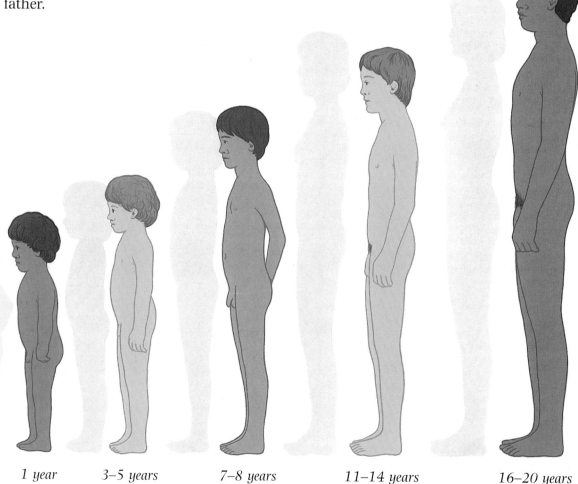

1 year   *3–5 years*   *7–8 years*   *11–14 years*   *16–20 years*

In boys and girls, the ▶
growth spurt during puberty
is based largely on the bones
of the skeleton. They
increase in size and length,
especially the long bones in
the upper arms, forearms,
thighs, and shins. The skull
also grows rapidly, giving an
angular, bony appearance to
the face. The small bones in
the wrists and ankles are the
last bones to become fully
grown and hardened. This
photo shows the bone
growth of a boy's hand at
two-and-a-half years (left),
six-and-a-half years (center),
and nineteen years (right).

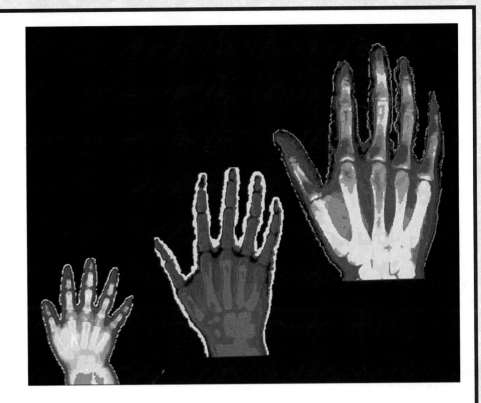

As in females, male puberty is part of the large-scale process of adolescence. This can involve great changes in attitudes, emotions, friendships, and relationships. An individual's experiences during adolescence partly depend on the local culture and traditions. In some societies, boys undertake some kind of test, or "rite of passage." If they succeed, from that day on they are regarded as fully grown men. In other places, maturing from boy to man is a long, drawn-out process.

◀ This chart shows the average height with age for boys in developed countries such as the United States. The growth spurt lags a couple of years behind that for girls, but on the average, final height is greater.

Depending on the personality and confidence of the boy or girl, it can be a period of embarrassment and worry or an enjoyable and fulfilling time.

The main changes of male puberty are under the control of the male hormone testosterone. They include
• rapid growth of the bones, with a rapid increase in height.
• development of the muscles, especially in the upper body.
• appearance of thicker, more conspicuous body hairs under the arms and between the legs (pubic hair), on the chest, and on the face—the beard and mustache.
• the growth of the male sexual organs, beginning with lengthening of the penis. This then becomes wider, too, and erections become more common. Gradually the testes also develop and begin to make sperm.
• breaking of the voice into a deeper tone. This usually happens during the later stages of puberty, at around 15 to 17 years.

Genes and Inheritance

Any complicated machine or structure, such as an airplane or skyscraper, needs a set of plans. All the parts are shaped and fitted according to the plans, so they work together properly. The human body also has a set of plans. They are in sections or units called genes, and there are between 100,000 and 200,000 for the body. Genes carry all the instructions needed for the body to develop from a fertilized egg, to grow into a baby, child, adolescent, and adult, and to maintain and repair itself.

What are genes? They are chemicals—molecules of the substance DNA (deoxyribonucleic acid). DNA is a very long, thin molecule, like two corkscrew-shaped parts twisted together. Along its length it has millions of sequences made from four subunits, called nucleic acids. The genetic information is carried in chemically-coded form, in the sequences of these subunits. (In a similar way, the letters of the alphabet can be arranged in different sequences into words and sentences, to convey information.)

Genes are found in every cell body. The lengths of DNA are coiled into objects called chromosomes. Under the microscope, these look like long threads inside the cell's nucleus (control center). There are 46 chromosomes in

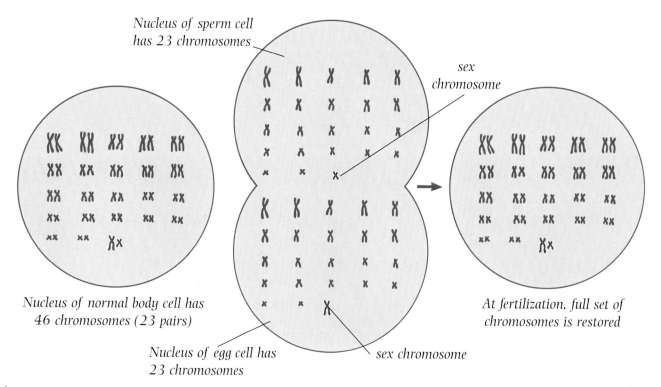

Nucleus of sperm cell has 23 chromosomes

sex chromosome

Nucleus of normal body cell has 46 chromosomes (23 pairs)

Nucleus of egg cell has 23 chromosomes

sex chromosome

At fertilization, full set of chromosomes is restored

▲ **There are two sets of chromosomes, one from the mother and one from the father.**

each cell. These 46 chromosomes are organized into 23 pairs. Originally, one member of each pair came from the mother, in the egg, and the other from the father, in the sperm. Every time a body cell divides, all the chromosomes are copied. This happens from the first cleavage of the fertilized egg to the day-to-day cell divisions in the skin, blood, and other body parts, as described below. That means every cell resulting from a cell division has the full set of 46 chromosomes.

Genes carry the same general information, but they differ in details, such as how tall the body will be, and its exact skin, eye, and hair color. That is why each person is unique. However, since the genes come from both father and mother, children also tend to resemble their parents. The passing on of features in the genes from parent to offspring is known as inheritance.

Body cells continually divide to replace those that wear out and die. The normal type of cell division is called mitosis. In mitosis, all 46 chromosomes (23 pairs), carrying between them all the genes in the form of lengths of DNA, are copied. So each of the two resulting cells gets a full set of chromosomes.

However, eggs in the ovary, and sperm in the testes, are made by a different type of cell division. This is called meiosis. The chromosomes are not copied. So each sperm or egg has only 23 chromosomes, one from each pair. When a sperm and an egg join at fertilization, their sets of 23 chromosomes come together, to restore the usual full number of 46. Also during meiosis the genes are shuffled so that each sperm or egg has a unique selection. That is why brothers and sisters have a general family likeness, but each is also different and unique.

▲ In this picture a scientist is analyzing the DNA from cells for different genes. Around the world, scientists are involved in the Human Genome Project. The genome is the full set of genes. The project aims to make a complete list of all the genes in a human and where they are on each chromosome. It will have great benefits in many areas, such as identifying inherited diseases.

FACT BOX

• DNA has only four "code letters"or nucleotide subunits. These are called adenine, thymine, guanine, and cytosine. All the genetic information is carried in sequences of these four in different orders.

• DNA is very long, but very thin. If it were enlarged to be as wide as a garden hose, an average DNA molecule would be 6 mi. (10 km) long.

• If all the DNA molecules in the 46 chromosomes of a single body cell were unraveled and joined end to end, they would stretch more than 6.5 ft. (2 m).

Diseases of the Reproductive System

Like other systems of the body, the reproductive system is at risk from diseases and medical conditions. Because of the system's close links and shared parts with the urinary system, an infection or problem in one can spread to the other.

The female and male reproductive systems have basic similarities. Each has a pair of glands that make the gametes or sex cells—eggs and sperm. In a woman, the glands are the ovaries, which produce eggs. In a man, the equivalent parts are the testes, which produce sperm. In each system a tube conveys the gametes away from the gland. In a woman, it is the oviduct (uterine tube or fallopian tube). In a man, it is the sperm duct (ductus deferens or vas deferens). However, there are also major differences between the male and female systems. That is why some diseases of the reproductive system affect only women, others affect only men, and some affect both men and women in similar ways.

Some people feel shy, embarrassed, or worried about health problems—and especially about a problem that may affect their genital organs or sexual parts. But in one very important way, such problems are the same as diseases elsewhere in the body. The sooner they are detected and medical advice is obtained, the better the chances are for effective treatment and cure. That is why doctors advise people to check themselves regularly, especially looking and feeling for lumps or changes, such as in the breast or testis. There are also clinics where a doctor or nurse can give checkups and specific advice.

Some of the more common conditions ▶ affecting the reproductive parts

▼ Regular checkups help identify problems at an early stage, when the chances of successful treatment are greater. This applies as much to the reproductive system as it does to the heart, lungs, and other body systems.

FEMALE

Menstrual problems are very varied, ranging from painful periods (dysmenorrhea) and/or heavy periods (menorrhagia), to infrequent and/or missing periods (oligomenorrhea). Treatments include pain-killing pills and hormone-containing tablets.

A breast lump may be a harmless cyst, an infection, an abscess, or rarely, some type of growth or tumor. That is why self-examination is important.

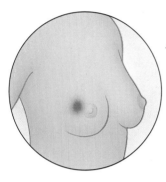

Ovarian cysts are fluid-filled bags or sacs that grow on or near the ovary. They are usually harmless and painless.

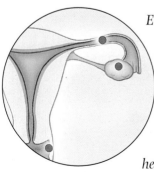

Endometriosis happens when parts of the inner lining of the uterus—the endometrium—lodge somewhere nearby. As the menstrual cycles proceed, these pieces grow and become blood-rich, causing pain and heavy periods.

MALE

Cancer of the testis is relatively rare, but it is one of the commonest cancers in men under the age of 40. It usually begins with a small lump or swelling in the affected testis. Detected early, there is an excellent chance of cure.

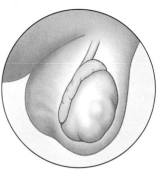

Undescended testes means the testes are still in the abdomen, where they develop in the early stages. Usually they descend or drop in the month before birth. An operation can correct the problem.

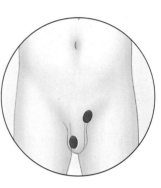

Enlarged prostate affects men over the age of 45–50 years. If the enlargement is severe, it can interfere with urination because it presses on the urine-carrying urethra that runs through it. There are several surgical methods to treat the problem.

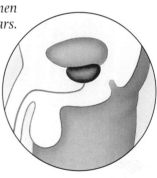

Balanitis is soreness, redness, pain, and swelling of the foreskin, at the end of the penis, and the underlying bulbous end of the penis, called the glans or balanus. It may be due to infection, irritating chemicals, contraceptive creams, or other substances in contact with the sensitive end of the penis.

Sexually Transmitted Diseases

Disease-causing microbes such as bacteria and viruses can spread from one person to another in many ways. They can float in the air or lodge in food that has been handled. They can be spread by physical contact between people such as by shaking hands and by sexual contact. Sexual contact includes the various forms of sex or sexual intercourse. It also includes contact that involves the sexual organs and other body parts, such as the genitals and the mouth, as in oral sex. (Mouth-to-mouth contact as in kissing is not usually included.)

Infections and diseases spread in this way are called sexually transmitted diseases (STDs). As with other infections, there is usually an incubation period, when a person has the germs and can pass them on to others, but the germs have not multiplied sufficiently or caused any symptoms or signs.

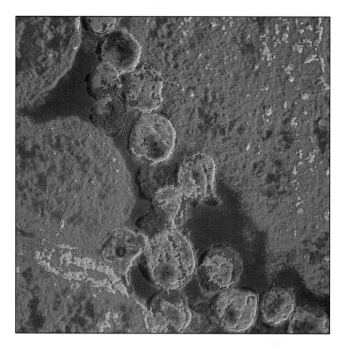

▲ **In this greatly enlarged photograph, taken through a microscope, the orange particles are HIVs—Human Immunodeficiency Viruses, the cause of the condition AIDS.**

FACT BOX

• The sure way of avoiding STDs is to avoid sexual intercourse or sexual contact.

• The infection is not always obvious in a sexual partner. He or she could be in the incubation period or latent ("quiet") stage of the infection, when there are no clear signs or symptoms.

• Using a condom (see page 45) can reduce the risk of transmission.

• A person who suspects he or she has caught an STD can go to the family doctor or to an STD clinic specializing in these conditions.

In some cases STDs cause not only health problems but also personal and social problems. If a person discovers that he or she has an STD, it is usually advisable to trace other people who have been in sexual contact with that person so they can receive medical advice and treatment, as necessary. This is called contact tracing. In some cases this is a matter of life and death, and it can prevent more people from being infected. However it also involves talking about sexual activity and sexual partners, which some people might wish to avoid—although all medical discussions are kept strictly private and confidential.

Sexually Transmitted Diseases

Name	Caused by	What happens	Treatment
AIDS, Acquired Immune Deficiency Syndrome	HIV, Human Immunodeficiency Virus	After a long incubation period, perhaps 10 years or more, the virus damages the body's immune system, so it cannot defend the body against infections and diseases. This causes fever, swollen glands, diarrhea, weight loss, infections such as pneumonia, cancer, mental confusion, many other conditions.	Some drugs may slow the progress of AIDS for a time; there is no known cure.
Syphilis	Bacteria called *Treponema pallidum*	There are several stages: first a sore or chancre where the germs entered the body, then a rash and skin warts, then possibly serious problems in the blood vessels, heart, and brain.	Antibiotic drugs
NSU, Non-Specific Urethritis	Various microbes such as *Chlamydia trachomatis*	The germs infect the urethra, which carries urine from the bladder to the outside, and cause tingling on urination and perhaps discomfort and a thick discharge from the urethra.	Antibiotic drugs
Gonorrhea	Bacteria called *Neisseria gonorrhoea*	The germs usually infect the urethra, which carries urine from the bladder to the outside, and other genital areas such as the cervix in women, causing some soreness and discharge.	Antibiotic drugs
Herpes (herpes genitalis)	Viruses called *Herpes simplex*, related to those that cause cold sores around the mouth	The virus causes blisters on the genital parts and nearby skin and swollen glands. The blisters burst and become painful ulcers or sores.	Pain-killing and anti-viral drugs
Trichomonas, or *trichomonal vaginitis*	A microbe called *Trichomonas vaginalis*, a protist or one-celled organism	The germ causes soreness and irritation of the genital area, especially of the vagina, and a thick, unpleasant-smelling discharge.	A course of pills
Pubic lice	Tiny crablike insects called lice	The lice infest the pubic hair, bite the skin to blood-suck, and cause itchy spots.	Special lotion, cream, or shampoo to kill the lice and their eggs, or nits, which attach to the hairs.

Fertility Problems and Treatments

Infertility is the condition of being unable to conceive a baby, after trying for some time—usually a year or more. A better name would be low fertility or delayed fertility, since many of the couples are able to find the cause of the problem, solve it, and then have a baby. Indeed, with modern medical techniques, more and more couples are being helped. True infertility, where there is never any chance of producing a baby, is increasingly rare.

There are many causes of lack of fertility. Some mainly involve the man, others are based on the woman, and some result from problems with both partners.

In the man, there may be too few sperm, which is called having a low sperm count. This in turn has many causes. They may include illness, stress, fatigue, alcohol abuse, and certain drugs. There may be a blockage or other abnormality in the testes or sperm ducts. The man may not be able to keep his penis erect for long enough during sexual intercourse. Or he may be unable to ejaculate the sperm from it. The sperm may be malformed. Or they may not swim in an active and healthy manner to reach the egg.

In the woman, hormonal and menstrual problems can mean that an egg does not ripen for release by the ovary. Or the oviduct (fallopian tube) may be blocked, so the egg cannot reach the uterus (and sperm cannot reach the egg). This may be due to previous infections or illnesses involving the reproductive organs. The lining of the uterus may not become thick and blood-rich, so the egg is fertilized but then it cannot implant into the lining. The problem may be a medical condition such as endometriosis. Another possibility is that the substances in the moist lining of the vagina and uterus may be very hostile to sperm, causing them to stop swimming or even die.

For each of these causes, there is usually a treatment. The numbers of male sperm can be boosted by hormones, medical drugs, or surgery to correct any abnormality. For a woman, surgery can repair certain blockages or abnormalities, and the ripening and release of eggs can also be treated by fertility drugs. There is also a variety of methods where sperm and/or eggs are removed from the body and then put back into the woman's body (see diagram).

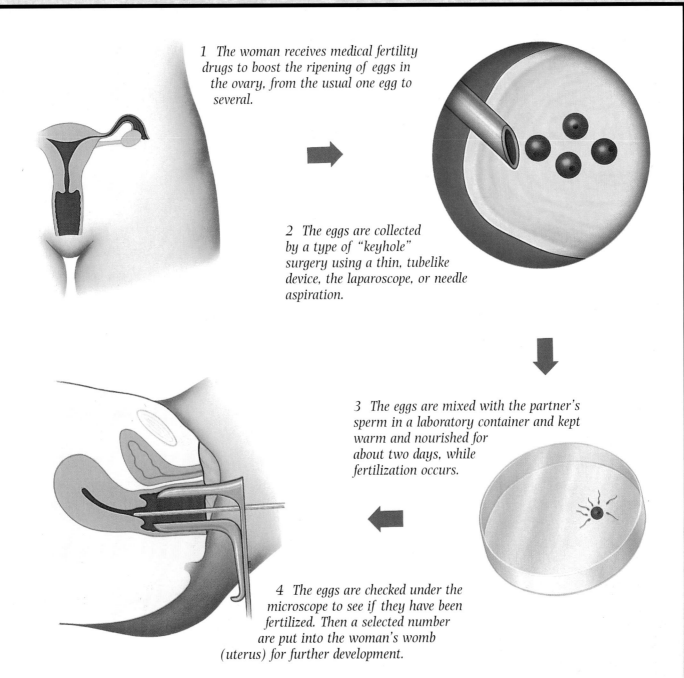

1 The woman receives medical fertility drugs to boost the ripening of eggs in the ovary, from the usual one egg to several.

2 The eggs are collected by a type of "keyhole" surgery using a thin, tubelike device, the laparoscope, or needle aspiration.

3 The eggs are mixed with the partner's sperm in a laboratory container and kept warm and nourished for about two days, while fertilization occurs.

4 The eggs are checked under the microscope to see if they have been fertilized. Then a selected number are put into the woman's womb (uterus) for further development.

One cause for lack of fertility may be that the couple do not fully understand the workings of the reproductive process. They may not realize how the sperm and eggs are made and released and the most effective times and ways to have sexual intercourse. They may not understand that the woman is able to conceive only around the time of egg release or ovulation (see page 8).

▲ Babies conceived by "in vitro" fertilization (IVF) are sometimes called test-tube babies, though there may not be any actual test tubes involved. *In vitro* means "in glass," and refers to the laboratory equipment such as glass dishes used for the technique. Another possible treatment is artificial insemination (AI), in which sperm are collected and inserted into the woman's vagina or uterus by using a special device or applicator.

Babies Around the World

The first half of this book shows that the biology of the reproductive system, and the reproductive cycle of sex, pregnancy, and birth, are much the same in humans as in other mammals. But our human intelligence makes reproduction much more complicated than it is for creatures in the wild.

For example, our closest relatives in the animal world are chimpanzees and gorillas. Their anatomy (body structure) and physiology (body function), including their reproductive systems, are extraordinarily similar to our own. Indeed, the genes of a human and chimp are about 99 percent identical. In chimps or gorillas, the mature females are usually pregnant with their unborn babies or breast-feeding their offspring on milk. It is rare to see a female who is capable of reproducing, but who is not involved directly in some stage of reproduction.

In humans, the emphasis is very different. There may be women of all ages who are not directly involved in reproduction, though they may have older children (who are no longer breast-feeding). In many societies, people have the knowledge about how reproduction happens. They can choose whether or not to have children—at least in theory. But there are usually constraints in the form of customs, traditions, moral and religious views; the expense of money and time; and the practical needs of everyday life.

◄ Some partners consult a doctor about how to improve their chances of having a baby. Others wish to do the opposite— avoid having a baby. They receive information on the various methods of contraception and choose the method that suits them best.

Factbox

 There are many forms of contraception. The choice of method is affected by many factors, such as personal preferences, religious and cultural views, and whether the method is readily available.

 • Calendar and rhythm methods rely mainly on the timing of sexual intercourse. Sex is avoided during the woman's most fertile time, around ovulation during the middle of the menstrual cycle.

• Most contraceptive pills work by altering the woman's menstrual cycle so that ripe eggs are not released from the ovary, and the lining of the uterus does not become thick and blood-rich. There are also implants that are put under the skin and stay effective for months, and "morning-after" pills for emergency use after unprotected sex.

 • Barrier methods involve putting a block or barrier in the path of the sperm, so they cannot reach the egg. They include the condom or sheath, which catches the sperm as they come out of the penis, and the diaphragm or cervical cap, which blocks the entry of sperm from the vagina into the uterus.

 • Chemical methods are mainly spermicides. These are substances that disable or destroy sperm, usually in the vagina. They may be creams, foams, jellies, or pessaries (vaginal suppositories), or they may be contained in a sponge. They are usually used in combination with other barrier methods.

 • IUDs, intrauterine devices (also called IUCDs or intrauterine contraceptive devices), are placed in the uterus or womb. There are various designs, including, coils, loops, Ts, and 7s. The presence of the IUD alters the lining of the uterus and prevents the egg from implanting.

In some cultures, parents want as many children as possible. It may be a sign of wealth and status to have a large family. In others, parents prefer to have just one or two children, or they may wish to have no children.

If people wish to avoid or limit their offspring, they may choose to avoid sex altogether. Or they can undergo surgery for sterilization, which means they can no longer release sperm or ripe eggs. They may choose to use contraception, which aims to prevent the conception of a baby after sexual intercourse.

If pregnancy occurs, they may choose termination (abortion), in which the embryo or early fetus is removed from the womb. Another option is adoption, where a baby or child leaves its natural mother and is raised by other people. If people wish to have children, but cannot, there are many medical techniques to improve their chances. These choices, whether to have children or not, involve altering the natural workings of the reproductive system and cycle.

Glossary

abdomen The part of the body containing the stomach, bowels, and reproductive organs

adolescence The physical developments of puberty plus associated emotional, social, and relationship changes. In humans, adolescence usually happens during the middle "teenage years."

cells Microscopic living units, the "building blocks" of the body, which consist of billions of different types of cells

cleavage The splitting or dividing of the fertilized egg cell into two cells, then four, eight, and so on

embryo The early growing and developing stage of a living thing, before birth or hatching. In humans, the embryonic stage is an eight-week stage after fertilization

fertilization Fertilization occurs when the male genetic material from the sperm joins with the female genetic material inside the egg

fetus The later stages in growth and development of a living thing, but still before birth or hatching. In humans, fetal growth happens in the period from eight to about 40 weeks after fertilization

follicle A bag- or saclike body part, usually small, soft, and filled mostly with fluid

glands Body parts that make and release a product, usually a fluid, that is useful to the body in some way

hormones Chemicals made in the body by parts called endocrine or hormonal glands, which control the activities of other parts called target organs

membrane A covering or lining, usually thin and flexible, that may cover a whole organ or just a single cell

mucus A sticky substance that forms the natural protective lining to the nose, mouth, reproductive tract, and other body parts

organs Fairly large, distinct parts of the body having major roles. The brain, heart, liver, testes, and ovaries are body organs.

ovary The female reproductive organ, which makes eggs and female sex hormones

ovulation Ovulation occurs when the ovary releases its ripe egg, which bursts out of its protective follicle

ovum The egg, the female reproductive cell, or gamete

puberty The time of rapid growth and development of a body, when it becomes sexually mature and able to reproduce (have offspring)

spermatozoon The sperm, the male reproductive cell, or gamete

testes The male reproductive organs. They make sperm and male sex hormones.

uterus (womb) The female organ or body part where the baby grows and develops before birth

Books to Read

Avraham, Regina. *The Reproductive System.* Healthy Body. New York: Chelsea House, 1991.

Bryan, Jenny. *Reproduction.* Body talk. Morristown, NJ: Silver Burdett Press, 1993.

Silverstein, Alvin. *Reproductive System.* Human Body Systems. New York: 21st Century Books, Inc., 1994.

Index